This Book Belongs To:

Gutsy Girl

gutsy \guht-see\ adjective: brave, courageous, daring.

Showing determination even when your heart beats fast, your hands grow sweaty, and you fear failure.

Dedications

To Ruby-Ru, my favorite scientist, may potions, paper clips, and floss always remind you of possibilities. —A.L.S.

To Alice, Lovell, Josi, and Jan, I love and adore you! —B.A.W.

Gutsy Girls: *Strong Christian Women Who Impacted the World*
Book Four: *Jennifer Wiseman*

ISBN-13: 978-1973976820

ISBN-10: 197397682X

Printed in the United States of America

Gutsy Girls

Strong Christian Women Who
Impacted the World

Book Four:
Dr. Jennifer Wiseman

Amy L. Sullivan

Illustrated by Beverly Ann Wines

Deep in the Ozark Mountains of Arkansas, young Jennifer lived on a farm.

Jennifer knew about God, and it was in nature that Jennifer discovered God's creativity.

"A shell to protect a turtle? Brilliant!"

"Underground caves decorated with stalactites? Beautiful!"

"A bug that crawls on top of water? You're kidding me!"

While exploring on the farm,
Jennifer became
interested
in . . .

animals,

rocks,

reuniting furry families,

Jesus,

and especially outer space.

One day while watching a television show, Jennifer learned about a moon of Jupiter with hundreds of erupting volcanoes.

"Volcanoes in space? How can this be?"

The idea of a volcano on a moon set Jennifer's imagination ablaze.

In the evenings, Jennifer walked with her parents and her dogs along quiet country roads. While her parents talked, Jennifer stared at the stars that stretched from horizon to horizon, and she imagined.

What would it be like to visit a star?
What would it be like to walk on the moon?
What would it be like to explore space?

Encouraged by her siblings, parents, teachers, and church, Jennifer
dedicated herself to learning more and more about space.
But she didn't keep that knowledge to herself.
Each time Jennifer learned something new,
she shared it with others.

"And now for your viewing enjoyment, it is my pleasure to present,

A BLACK HOLE!"

Jennifer learned that there are hundreds of billions of galaxies in the universe with hundreds of billions of stars in each galaxy. She also learned that stars aren't just beautiful to look at. They're God's factories, and He uses them to create what we need to live. The more Jennifer learned, the more she knew God had been very, very busy sculpting the universe.

Jennifer also learned Psalm 19:1: "The heavens declare the glory of God; the skies proclaim the work of His hands."

While she was in college, Jennifer and her colleague Brian discovered a comet, later named 114P/Wiseman-Skiff. This comet comes back into view every six and a half years and looks like a big, dirty snowball that forms a tail as it comes closer to the earth and the sun.

Throughout her life, Jennifer met others who thought people needed to choose between science and God. Jennifer thought this idea was sillier than a sunny day on Neptune.

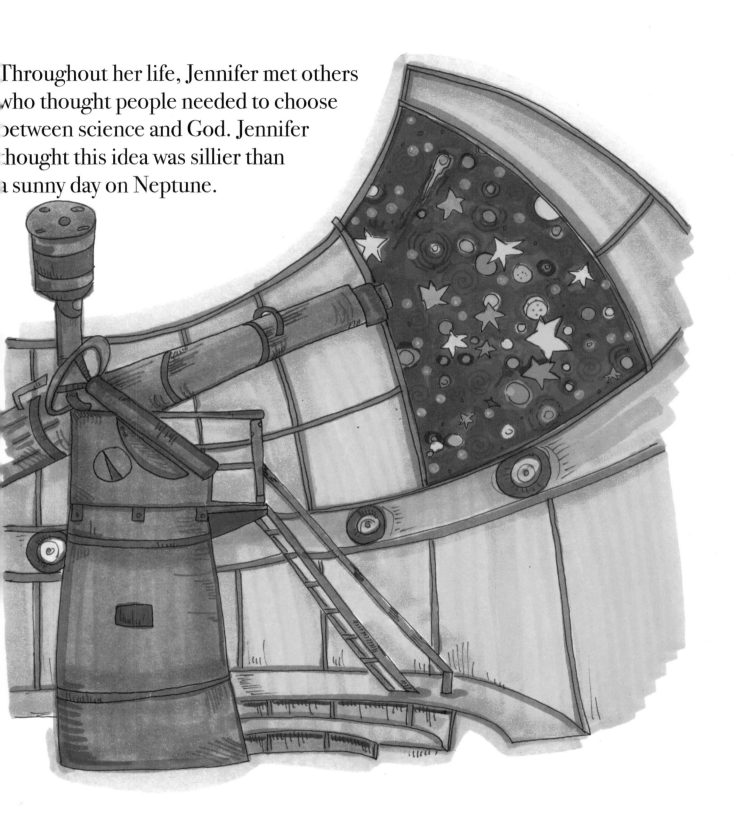

She knew that everything we learn from science shows us God's stunning handiwork.

Today Jennifer works with a variety of telescopes, some on the ground and some in space, which take pictures of planets, stars, and colorful clouds between stars. She travels to share what she learns with other scientists, students, and people everywhere.

Jennifer also leads conversations about God and science. She has made it her life's work to be curious and explore God's creation. While studying the universe, Jennifer discovered the depth of God's power, patience, love, and creativity.

While some people look only to science to answer hard questions, Jennifer knows science was never meant to answer all our questions.

Why did God make the universe so Big?

How many galaxies and stars are

Why aren't all the planets the same?

How did God come up with the idea for gravity?

Why are we in the universe?

Did God put any other kinds of life on other planets?

What's inside a black hole?

Why do astronauts feel weightless in space?

Even with all her knowledge about science and space, Jennifer knows that the most important truth doesn't come from searching skies, reading books, or experimenting in laboratories. Instead, it comes from a relationship with God. Jennifer understands that the God who filled the heavens with stars is the same God who knows, loves, and guides her.

That's gutsy.

Why did God make the universe so Big?

How many galaxies and stars are the same?

Why aren't all the planets the same?

What in the universe?

Did God put any other kinds of life on other planets?

How did God come up with the idea for gravity?

What's inside a black hole?

How do astronauts feel weightless in space?

Words for Gutsy Girls

1. ablaze - being on fire or radiant with emotion.

2. black hole - an object in space that is so dense it creates an enormous gravitational pull that can even pull in light. Objects in space, which are too close, get pulled in.

3. erupting - to break open with strong force.

4. galaxy - a large system of stars and planets.

5. horizon - an imaginary line separating the earth and sky.

6. Ozark Mountains - a mountain range, which stretches primarily through Arkansas, Missouri, and Oklahoma.

7. stalactites - a deposit of calcium carbonate which looks like an icicle hanging from the top or sides of a cave.

Sources

Bailey, Sarah Pulliam. "50 Women You Should Know." *Christianity Today*. Christianity Today, 19 Oct. 2012. Web. 2 Sept. 2015.

Brumfiel, Geoff. "After 25 Years, The Hubble Space Telescope Still Wows Humanity." *Npr*. Npr, 24 Apr. 2015. Web. 15 Sept. 2015.

Gutro, Rob. "A 25th Anniversary Q&A about Hubble with NASA's Jennifer Wiseman." *NASA*. Ed. Lynn Jenner. NASA, 28 Apr. 2015. Web. 1 Sept. 2016.

Test of FAITH: Does Science Threaten Belief in God? John Templeton Foundation, 1 Sept. 2010. Web. 10 Sept. 2016.

Wiseman, Jennifer. Message to the author. 21 Sept. 2016. E-mail.

Wiseman, Jennifer. Message to the author, 8 May 2017. E-mail.

Wiseman, Jennifer. Message to the author, 25 May 2017. E-mail.

Wiseman, Jennifer. Message to the author, 3 June 2017. E-mail.

Wiseman, Jennifer. Message to the author, 16 June 2017. E-mail.

Wiseman, Jennifer. Message to the author, 25 June 2017. E-mail.

Historical Note on Dr. Jennifer Wiseman

Real-life gutsy girl Dr. Jennifer Wiseman is an astronomer and astrophysicist. She studies stars and interstellar clouds using radio, infrared, and optical telescopes. Jennifer has worked with several major astronomy observatories over her career including the National Radio Astronomy Observatory and the National Aeronautics and Space Administration's (NASA) Hubble Space Telescope. However, before Dr. Wiseman worked as a leader in science, she was a kid just like you!

Born on April 2, 1965, Jennifer is the youngest of four children. As a child, while Jennifer explored the creek that ran through her family's farm, she found minnows, crawdads, frogs, and a deep love for God's creation. In the summer, Jennifer swam in a lake and wandered around meadows observing deer, squirrels, and rabbits. In the winter, Jennifer fed birds and participated in her all-time favorite childhood activity, snow hiking!

Though Jennifer developed a love for science as a young girl, she loved Jesus even more. Jennifer belonged to a loving church where she learned about God's great love at a very young age. Her two favorite accounts in the Bible are the birth of Jesus and His resurrection. In each case, Jennifer loved hearing how God shined light into the lives of His people by sending His son, Jesus.

By the time Jennifer reached high school, she was almost six feet tall. She played basketball, participated in the marching band's flag team, threw discus, and even mastered the clarinet.

Today Jennifer works hard to help people learn about space and about God. She does this by sharing what she learns with scientists and students everywhere.

Your Turn

Do you want to try the black hole experiment illustrated in this book? Grab a parent, and head to NASA's Afterschool Universe YouTube channel to watch the "Afterschool Universe: Creating a Black Hole" episode at https://www.youtube.com/watch?v=pcOxhdu5gh8.

Gutsy Girls
Strong, Christian Women Who Impacted the World

Book One: Gladys Aylward

Book Two: Sisters, Corrie and Betsie ten Boom

Book Three: Fanny Crosby

Book Four: Dr. Jennifer Wiseman

Book Five: Sojourner Truth

For free educational materials for classrooms, churches, and families, visit the author's website, AmyLSullivan.com.

About the Author

Amy L. Sullivan doesn't always feel brave, but her picture book series, *Gutsy Girls: Strong Christian Women Who Impacted the World*, allows her to comb through history and steal wisdom from the great women who came before her. Amy lives with her handsome husband, two daughters, naughty dog, and lazy cat in the mountains of Western North Carolina. Connect with Amy at AmyLSullivan.com.

About the Illustrator

Beverly Ann Wines is an illustrator, painter, and art teacher. Beverly's art reflects who she is and what she loves. Beverly's art can be found in bookstores, homes, and galleries across the nation. You can learn more about Beverly's work by emailing her at Bvrlywines@aol.com or visiting her website beverlysartandsoul.weebly.com.

CPSIA information can be obtained
at www.ICGtesting.com
Printed in the USA
BVHW021306210319
543341BV00010B/52/P